THE BIRTHDAY OF GURU NANAK

By
Shalini Vallepur

BookLife PUBLISHING

©2019
BookLife Publishing Ltd.
King's Lynn
Norfolk, PE30 4LS

All rights reserved.
Printed in Malaysia.

A catalogue record for this book is available from the British Library.

ISBN: 978-1-78637-806-4

Written by:
Shalini Vallepur

Edited by:
Madeline Tyler

Designed by:
Drue Rintoul

All facts, statistics, web addresses and URLs in this book were verified as valid and accurate at time of writing. No responsibility for any changes to external websites or references can be accepted by either the author or publisher.

CONTENTS

Words that look like this can be found in the glossary on page 24.

CELEBRATE THE BIRTHDAY OF GURU NANAK WITH ME!

Happy Guru Nanak Gurpurab!
My name is Mandeep.
I'm here to tell you about
Guru Nanak's birthday so
you can celebrate it with me.

Gurpurab is the **Punjabi** word for a Guru's birthday.

We celebrate Guru Nanak Gurpurab when there is a full moon in late October or November. It is a time for families and the <u>community</u> to come together.

SIKHISM

Guru Nanak Gurpurab is a celebration that is part of a religion called Sikhism. Sikhism began in the Punjab. Today, the Punjab is in India and Pakistan.

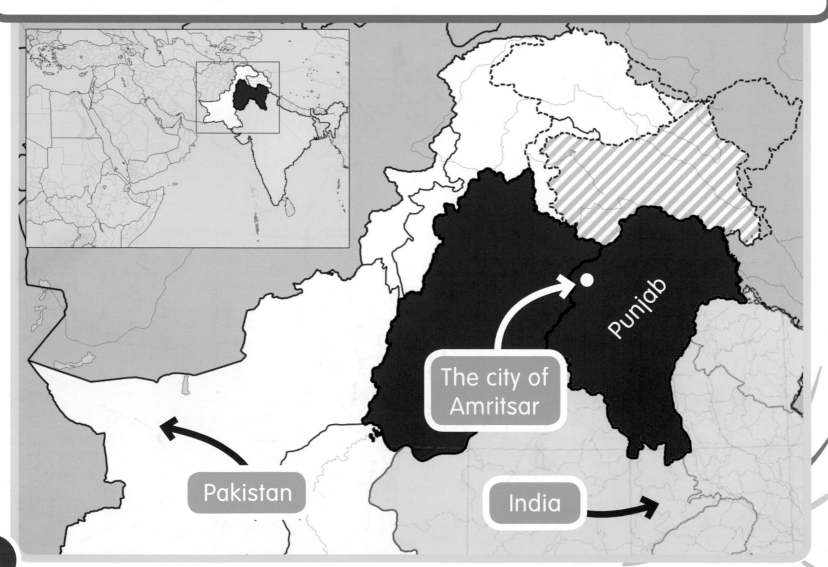

The city of Amritsar

Punjab

Pakistan

India

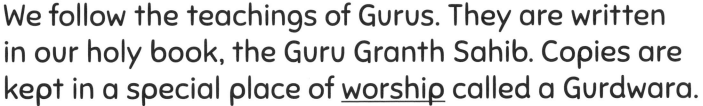

We follow the teachings of Gurus. They are written in our holy book, the Guru Granth Sahib. Copies are kept in a special place of <u>worship</u> called a Gurdwara.

This Gurdwara in Amritsar is known as the Golden Temple.

GURU NANAK

There have been ten Gurus in the past, and Guru Nanak was the first. He believed that there is only one God and that everybody is the same no matter who they are or where they come from.

'Guru' means teacher.

Guru Nanak Gurpurab is a special day for Sikhs, as Guru Nanak started the religion of Sikhism.

THE STORY OF GURU NANAK

Guru Nanak was born to a Hindu family in the year 1469. As he grew up, he learnt a lot about the religions Hinduism and Islam. He was very clever and was good at poetry and <u>philosophy</u>.

One day, Nanak went to a river to bathe. He did not come back for three days. During his time away, Nanak was speaking with God.

Nanak became Guru Nanak and he began to <u>practise</u> Sikhism. He travelled far and wide to spread Sikhism.

He spread the belief that there is one God and that everybody is the same. He also taught people that they should lead a good life and that they should pray to God.

AKHAND PATH

The Akhand Path begins two days before Guru Nanak Gurpurab. This is where the Guru Granth Sahib is read aloud for two days without stopping.

Reading the Guru Granth Sahib is important because we remember all the lessons from the Gurus. We feel connected to them and to Guru Nanak.

NAGAR KIRTAN

The day before Guru Nanak Gurpurab is Nagar Kirtan. This is a <u>procession</u> that happens in the streets early in the morning. There are lots of <u>floats</u> in the procession. The Guru Granth Sahib is carried on a float.

The procession is led by five Sikh men called the Panj Piare. Holy songs called shabad are sung and we all join in.

There is so much to see during the procession. Sikh soldiers and specially trained people use swords or sticks and pretend to fight. It is a brilliant show.

Everybody comes to the procession. Old or young, rich or poor, everybody is welcome. We feel at peace with each other as we sing. Soon, we reach the Gurdwara and the Guru Granth Sahib is taken inside.

GURU NANAK GURPURAB

The next day is Guru Nanak's birthday. The day starts early in the morning with shabad and then <u>meditation</u>.

After this it is time for langar. This is a special lunch for the whole community. Food is cooked by <u>volunteers</u>. Everybody can come to the Gurdwara and eat a free lunch.

FESTIVE FOOD

We always eat roti during langar. Roti is a round flatbread that we eat with foods such as curry. Volunteers make and cook the roti for everyone.

We are also given a sweet food called karah parshad. It is made from flour, sugar and butter. This food is very important because it is a gift from the Gurdwara and the Gurus.

Karah parshad

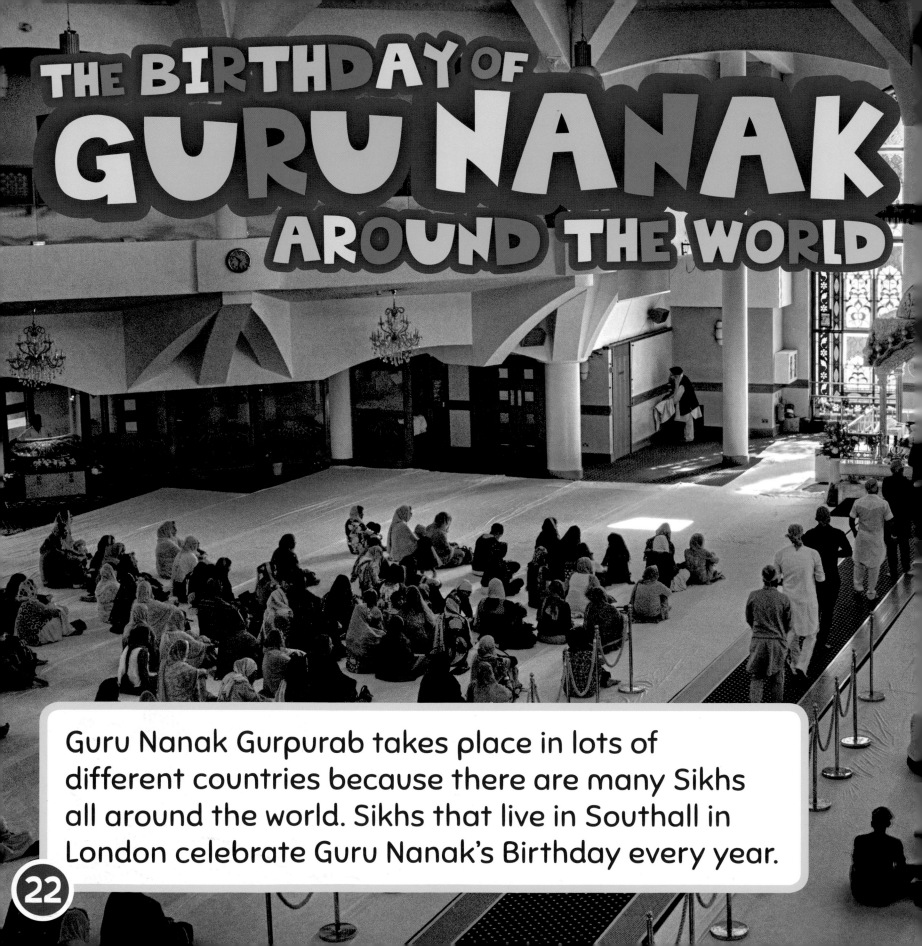

THE BIRTHDAY OF GURU NANAK AROUND THE WORLD

Guru Nanak Gurpurab takes place in lots of different countries because there are many Sikhs all around the world. Sikhs that live in Southall in London celebrate Guru Nanak's Birthday every year.

I hope you've learnt a lot about Guru Nanak's birthday and why we celebrate it. Why not see if there are any celebrations where you live?

GLOSSARY

community	a group of people who are connected by something
floats	small platforms on a moving cart or car used in processions
meditation	focusing the mind, often in silence and usually for religious or relaxation purposes
philosophy	learning and studying life, knowledge and lots of important human topics
practise	to do something
procession	a line of people or vehicles moving forwards
Punjabi	a language from the Punjab region spoken in Pakistan and India
volunteers	people that work or help without being paid
worship	a religious act where a person shows their love for a god

INDEX

24